In My Lunchbox

written by Pam Holden

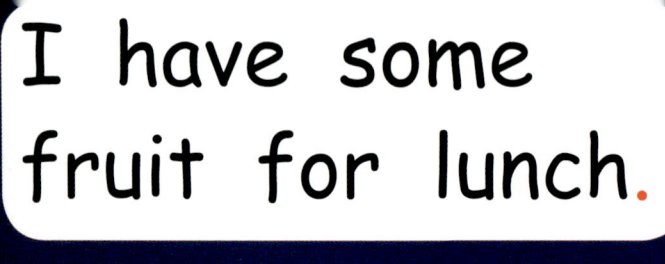

I have some fruit for lunch.

I have a banana in my lunchbox.

I have a sandwich for lunch.

I have tomato in my sandwich.

I have a drink in my lunchbox.

I have a pear, too.

I have some yoghurt for lunch.

I have a muffin, too.

I have an orange in my lunchbox.

I have some cheese, too.

I have some corn for lunch.

I have some grapes, too.

I have an apple in my lunchbox.

I have some pizza, too.

I have some watermelon. Yum!